Shakespeare's World

Includes music from the classic feature films:
Romeo & Juliet, Hamlet, and Henry V

Arranged by Richard Harris

© 1998 by Faber Music Ltd
First published in 1998 by Faber Music Ltd
3 Queen Square, London WC1N 3AU
Music set by Chris Hinkins
Cover by S & M Tucker
Printed in England by Halstan & Co Ltd
All rights reserved

ISBN 0 571 51907 5

To buy Faber Music publications or to find out about the full range of titles available
please contact you local music retailer or Faber Music sales enquiries:

Tel: +44(0) 171 833 7931
Fax: +44 (0) 171 833 7930
E-mail: sales@fabermusic.co.uk
Website://www.fabermusic.co.uk

FABER ***ff*** MUSIC

CONTENTS

Front Cover: *A Midsummer Night's Dream*, pub. by Currier and Ives, New York (litho)
by N. Currier (1813-88) & Ives, J.M. (1824-95) (after) Museum of the City of New York/
Bridgeman Art Library, London/New York.

ROMEO AND JULIET
The First Kiss

Nellee Hooper, Craig Armstrong, Marius de Vries

MUCH ADO ABOUT NOTHING
Sigh No More, Ladies

Patrick Doyle

HENRY V (Kenneth Branagh)
Opening Titles

Patrick Doyle

8

HENRY V (Laurence Olivier)
Death of Falstaff (Passacaglia)

William Walton

Molto lento

The Winter's Tale
Amor Est in Pectore

Nigel Hess

OTHELLO
Willow Song

Nigel Hess

A MIDSUMMER NIGHT'S DREAM
Wedding March

Felix Mendelssohn

HAMLET (Kenneth Branagh)
Death of Hamlet

Patrick Doyle

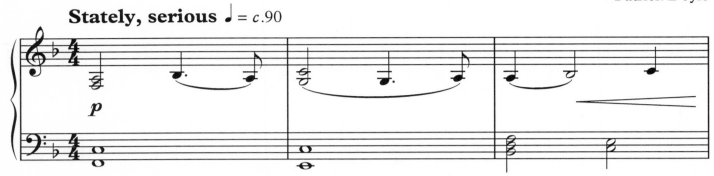

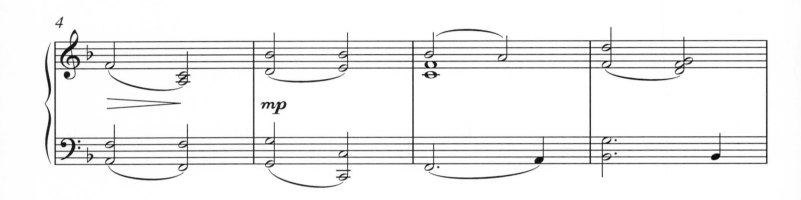

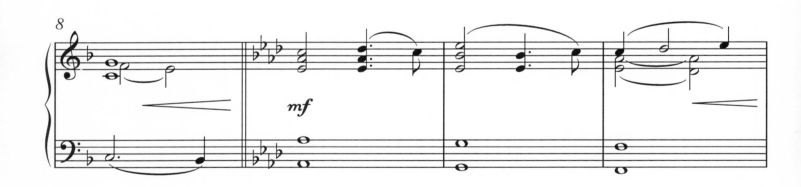

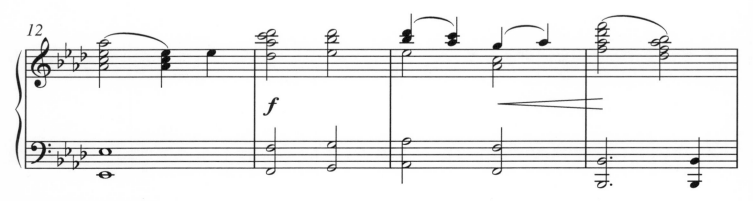

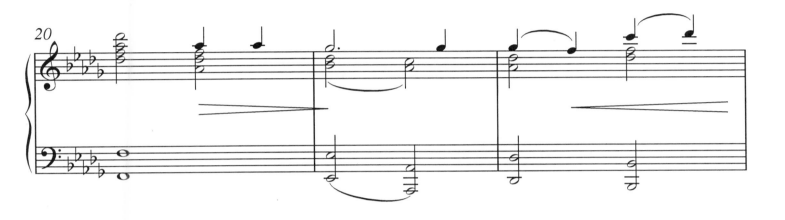

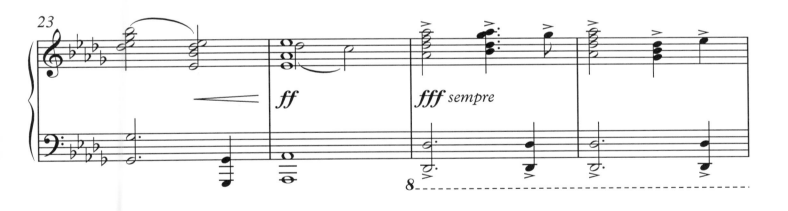

THE TEMPEST
Where the Bee Sucks

Stephen Warbeck

ROMEO AND JULIET
Fantasy Overture

Pyotr Ilyich Tchaikovsky

22

HAMLET (Franco Zeffirelli)
End Titles

Ennio Morricone

TWELFTH NIGHT
Drinking Scene
(Sir Andrew Aguecheek & Sir Toby Belch)

Richard Harris